Communication FUNdamentals

written and illustrated by
Jean Morrison

Bear With Me Press

Santa Cruz, California
Copyright 2017 by Jean Morrison
ISBN 978-0-9986184-0-1

This book is dedicated to all of my teachers and fellow students of Nonviolent Communication (NVC) and to the founder of this work, Marshall B. Rosenberg. His first comment when scanning this book was, "I always wanted to write one like this too." (Please read his internationally-acclaimed book, Nonviolent Communication, A Language of Life.)

I hope what you discover in these pages will contribute to your quality of life and conversations, and to peaceful co-existence with each person.

jean morrison

Welcome to
Communication FUNdamentals !

This book is a tool for learning Nonviolent Communication (NVC);
also called Compassionate Communication, or
"A Language of Life."

NVC was developed by Marshall B. Rosenberg, Ph.D.,
who devoted his life to understanding the roots of violence,
and how to heal and invite connection
through empathy and compassion.
NVC is currently taught in five continents
by hundreds of trainers and practitioners.

Who is learning NVC?

Individuals, couples, families, organizations, governments,
and groups such as:
students, educators, health care professionals, counselors, therapists,
scientists, attorneys, corporate teams, inmates, correctional officers,
business people, social activists, tribal members,
philosophers, artists, spiritual and religious leaders.
The list goes on.....

Why do people want to learn NVC?

To:
- Better understand themselves and others
- Get along with others, be heard and to hear each other
- Live more harmoniously and respectfully
- Heal old wounds and help prevent new ones
- Speak up honestly and listen compassionately
- Have more fun, joy, and peace

CONTENTS

KEY:

Thinking

Talking

NVC Circle of Life

The diagram demonstrates:
• Jackal "habitual" language outside the circle
• Giraffe "natural" language inside the circle

When we use Jackal language silently or out loud it can alienate us from others and from our own quality of life.

We can consciously use *intention, connection, choice, freedom* (forming the rim of the circle) to shift ourselves from Jackal habits outside the circle to Giraffe choices within the circle.

When we're speaking or listening with conscious awareness of *observations, feelings, needs, and requests,* we can enrich our own and others' lives.

 Living the language of Giraffe helps create balance and wholeness, and supports an intention to serve and to celebrate life.

judgments
labels
interpretations
evaluations

expectations
blame
"shoulds"
"shouldn'ts"

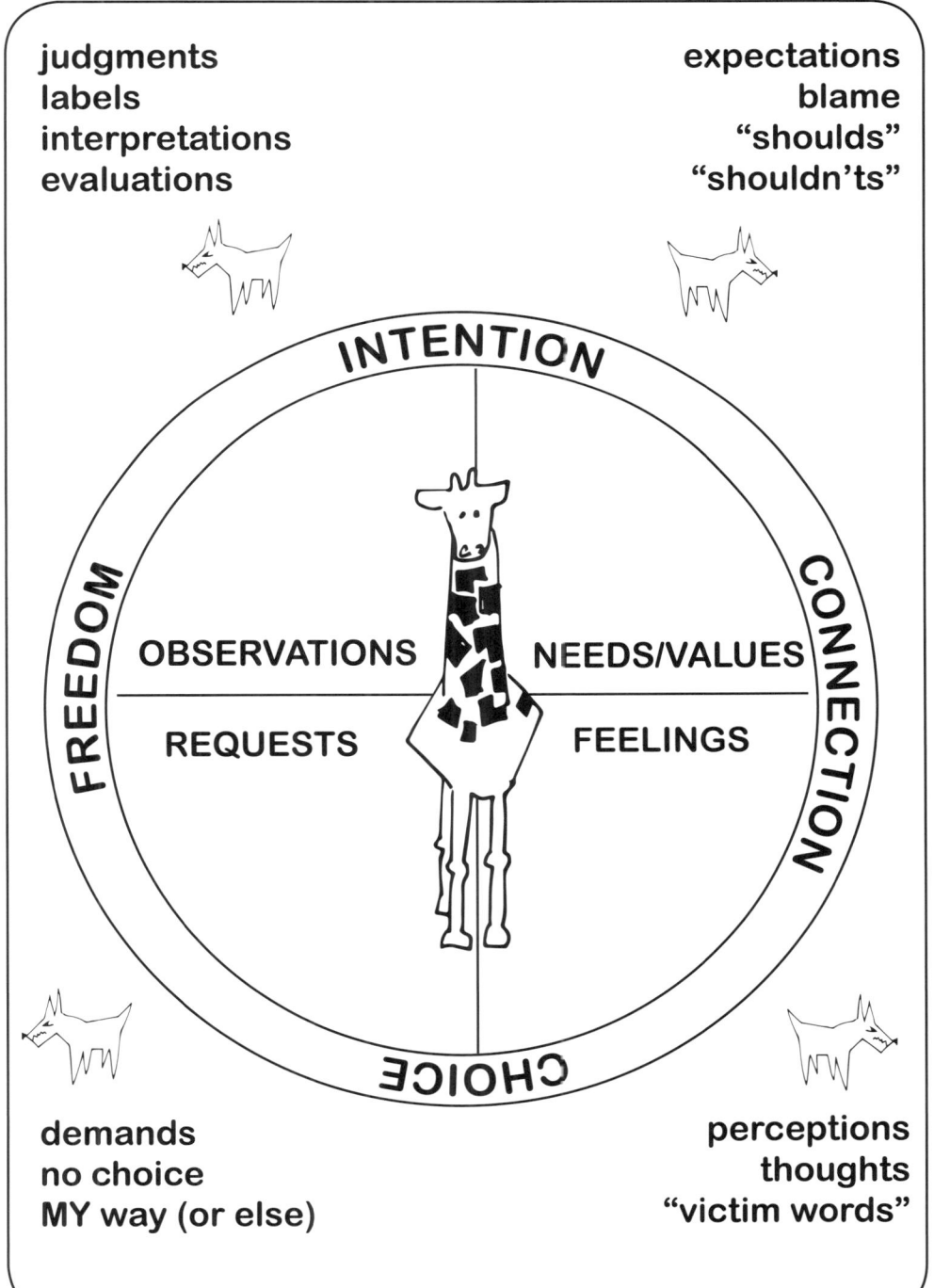

INTENTION

FREEDOM

CONNECTION

OBSERVATIONS   NEEDS/VALUES

REQUESTS   FEELINGS

CHOICE

demands
no choice
MY way (or else)

perceptions
thoughts
"victim words"

1

JACKAL **DISTINCTIONS**

I'm a symbol representing the habitual pattern of attack, defend, or run away.

GIRAFFE **DISTINCTIONS**

I'm a symbol representing the natural pattern of speaking and listening from the heart with a big perspective.

JACKAL **MOTIVATIONS**

- *To change another*
- *To control another*
- *To punish another*
- *To get my own way*

JACKAL is used to represent that part of us which
blames, attacks, and/or runs away.

JACKAL language and behavior alert us to look
deeper for the underlying feelings, needs,
and values in self and in others.

...just as a flashing warning-light on the dashboard
of our car alerts us to look under the hood
to see what is needed.

GIRAFFE **MOTIVATIONS**

- *To enrich life*
- *To connect with self & with others*
- *To be self-responsible*
- *To create mutual understanding*

GIRAFFE is used to represent the part of us which
is authentic and compassionate.

GIRAFFE language and behavior affirm
we are taking responsibility
for our feelings, needs, and actions,
and we are caring for others in the same way.

...symbolized by the giraffe's very large heart
(averaging 27 lbs.),
and it's height (averaging 16'), giving it a
tall perspective of life around it.

LIFE-ALIENATING

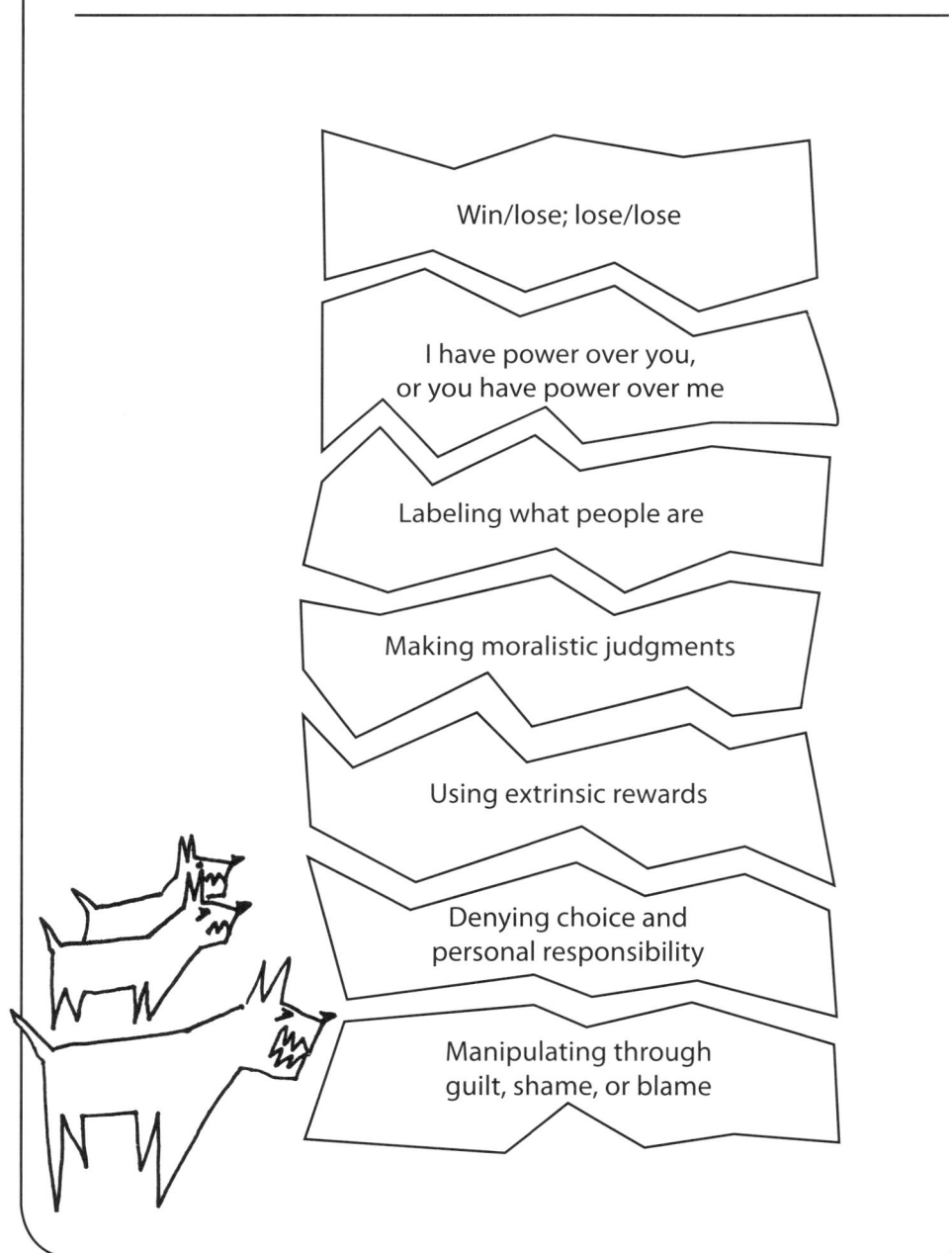

Win/lose; lose/lose

I have power over you,
or you have power over me

Labeling what people are

Making moralistic judgments

Using extrinsic rewards

Denying choice and
personal responsibility

Manipulating through
guilt, shame, or blame

LIFE-SERVING

Win/win

Power with others

How people are

Value judgments

Intrinsic reward

Personal
responsibility

Strategies that
mutually meet needs

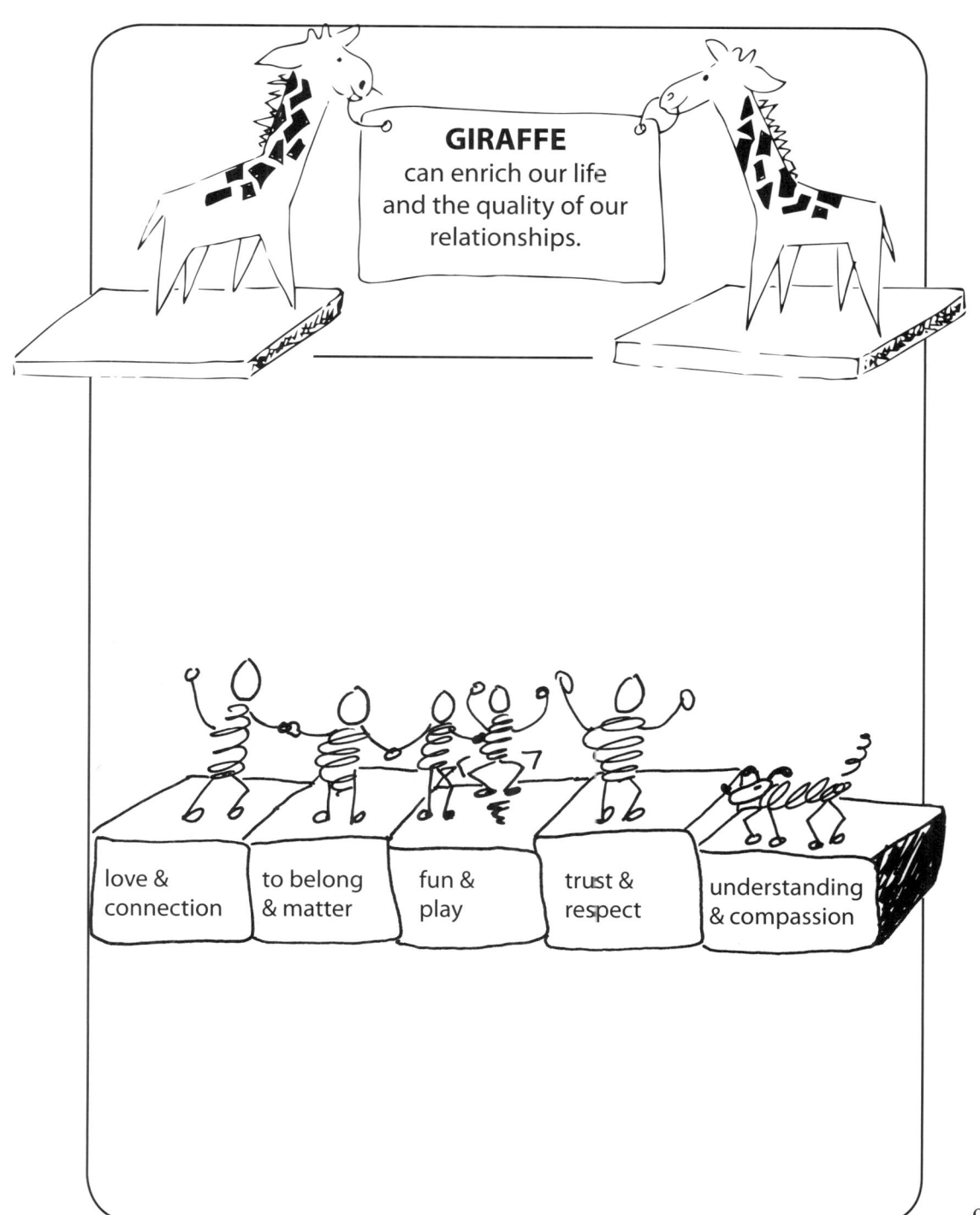

JACKAL **GUIDE**

GIRAFFE **GUIDE**

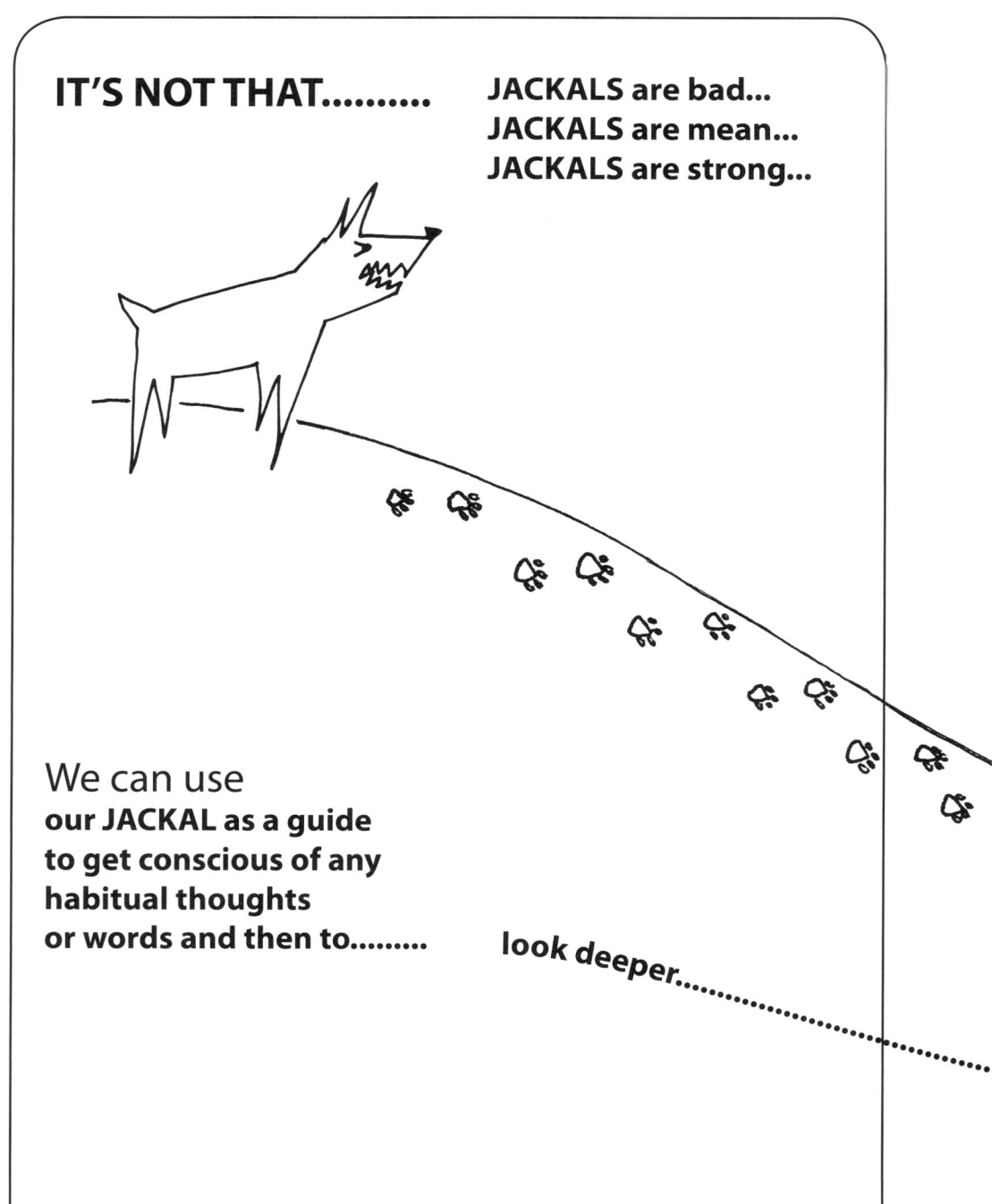

IT'S NOT THAT..........   JACKALS are bad...
JACKALS are mean...
JACKALS are strong...

We can use
**our JACKAL as a guide
to get conscious of any
habitual thoughts
or words and then to.........** **look deeper.....................**

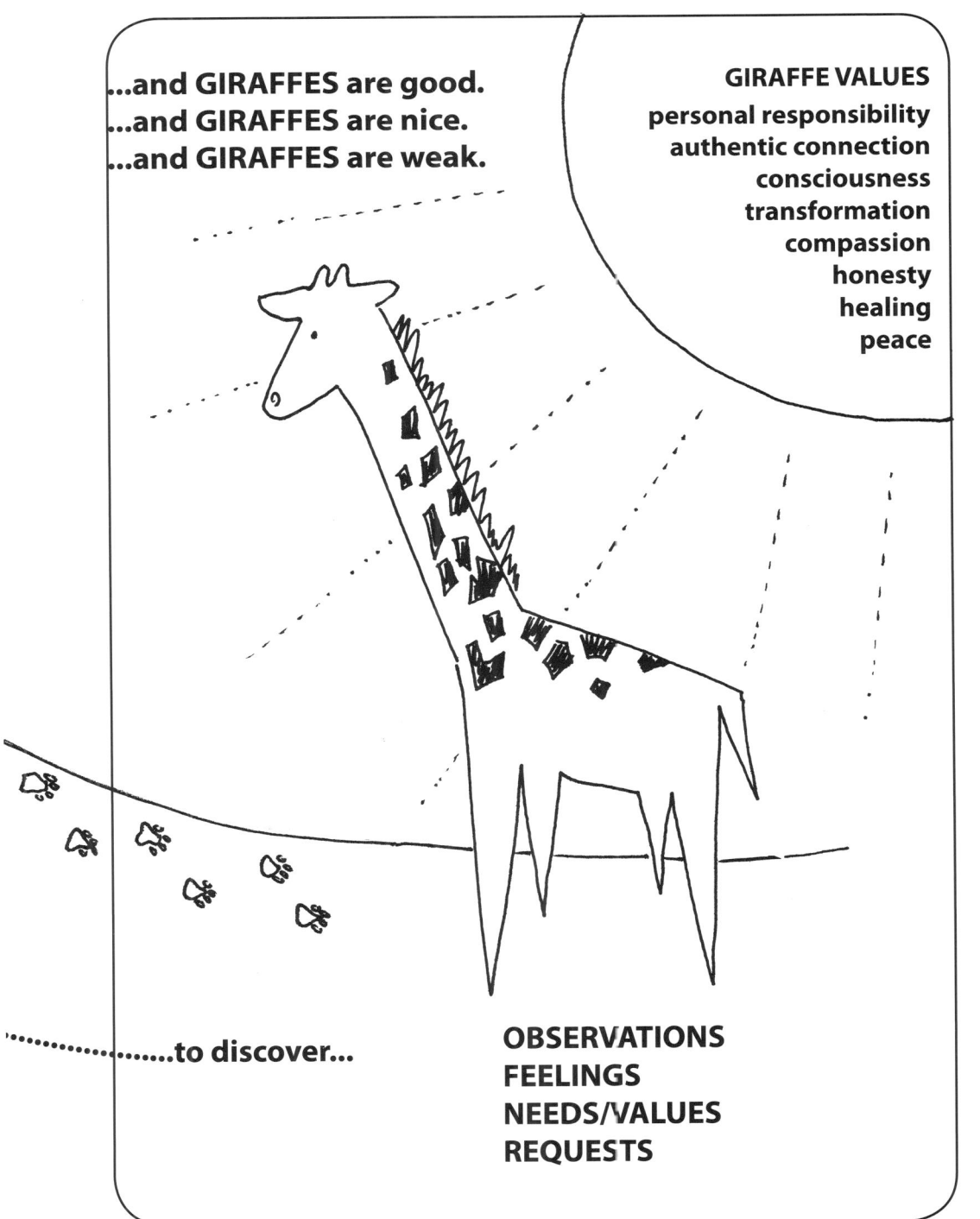

JACKAL **LANGUAGE USES**
labels, evaluations, accusations, judgments, assumptions, criticism, and interpretations

JACKAL **FALSE FEELINGS**
Express a thought, perception, or belief of what I think
someone is doing to me (my victim thinking)

abandoned	cornered	let down	rejected
abused	criticized	lied to	smothered
attacked	disrespected	manipulated	trapped
betrayed	dominated	neglected	tricked
blamed	dumped on	overworked	harassed
bullied	forced	patronized	unheard
cheated	hassled	provoked	unseen
coerced	ignored	put down	used
controlled	left out	put upon	violated

I'm feeling unappreciated.

You're disrespecting me!

I think you're bullying me!

GIRAFFE **TRUE FEELINGS**
Emotions when my needs/values are satisfied

comfortable	excited	loving	joyful
rested	enthusiastic	appreciative	exuberant
content	happy	affectionate	cheerful
relaxed	optimistic	tender	lively
nourished	amused	curious	fascinated
peaceful	jazzed	hopeful	adventurous
relieved	energetic	inspired	
fulfilled	pleased	grateful	
satisfied	glad	delighted	
calm	mischievous	confident	

I feel content.

emotions when I'm wanting to satisfy my needs/values

uncomfortable	tired	scared
uneasy	torn	afraid
mad	sad	worried
irritable	unhappy	anxious
grumpy	depressed	helpless
impatient	lonely	terrified
angry	miserable	insecure
hurt	gloomy	horrified
bitter	regretful	shocked
resentful	hopeless	suspicious
confused	jealous	embarassed
indifferent	skeptical	nervous
troubled	bored	puzzled

I feel worried.

JACKAL
uses **habitual strategies** mistaken for needs

- to get even
- to control you
- to have power over you
- to give you power over me
- to complain and whine
- to feel sorry for myself
- to be right (all the time!)
- to make others feel guilty, inferior, stupid, envious, jealous
- to blame you, anyone, everyone, God, myself

- to punish you
- to correct you
- to manipulate you
- to hold a grudge
- to be a martyr

GIRAFFE
connects to universal **NEEDS/VALUES**

SURVIVAL
air • food
water • sleep
shelter • touch

_____

SAFETY
security
protection
predictability
consistency
order

AUTONOMY
choice
competence
ability
self-expression
creativity
privacy

_____

HARMONY
peace
order
spirituality
nature
beauty
well-being

ENRICH LIFE
contribution
goals
meaning
purpose
unity
compassion
celebration
mourning
synergy
discovery
empowerment
equality

learning

COMMUNITY
connection
belonging
friendship
love, care
attention
intimacy
comfort
acceptance
to matter
to be seen
to be heard
help support
sharing
acknowledgment
interdependence
co-operation

How JACKALS **relate to** the word "NEEDS"

- People are so needy!
- I don't have needs
- I need you to _____.
- I need you to be _____.
- My needs don't matter.
- My needs are too much.

How GIRAFFES relate to the word "NEEDS"

- Needs, values, wants, wishes, hopes, dreams, life energy, "the juicy parts of life"
- What humans care about and seek fulfillment for
- I can sense in my body when I'm connected to needs - either to celebrate or mourn

JACKAL **BLAMES OTHERS**

for needs not getting met

GIRAFFE **TAKES RESPONSIBILITY**
for own feelings and needs

JACKAL language **MAKES DEMANDS**
Examples of unconscious
THINKING that creates demands

I expect others to do what I think is right or appropriate.

I keep trying, even using manipulation, to get my own way.

I want to control the outcome. My way or the highway!

I'm stuck in only one stragegy -- mine!

I made a reasonable request and you should say YES! I have a strong resistance to hearing a NO!

GIRAFFE language **MAKES REQUESTS**
Examples of conscious
THINKING that create requests

I want to connect with you and stay connected with myself at the same time.

I value your needs as equal to mine, although our timing and priorities may differ.

I will take protective action only if health or safety is at risk.

I want us to find a win/win solution.

I'm open to hearing a NO as well as to discovering what you're feeling and wanting.

JACKAL **DEMANDS**

- a real or implied threat of unpleasant consequences if the person does not comply
- mixing up needs with strategies

GIRAFFE **REQUESTS**

- doable, specific, present actions
- negotiable strategies to meet needs/values

JACKAL **DEMANDS**
are often met with

I need you to take me to the airport tonight.

Submission
"Well, OK, I guess I could leave work early."

Rebellion
"You could get there yourself! What's your problem?"

Defiance
"No way! Who made me your slave?!"

GIRAFFE **REQUESTS**
are more easily met with

Honesty & Choice
"I'm working late tonight, so I'm unable to help you out."

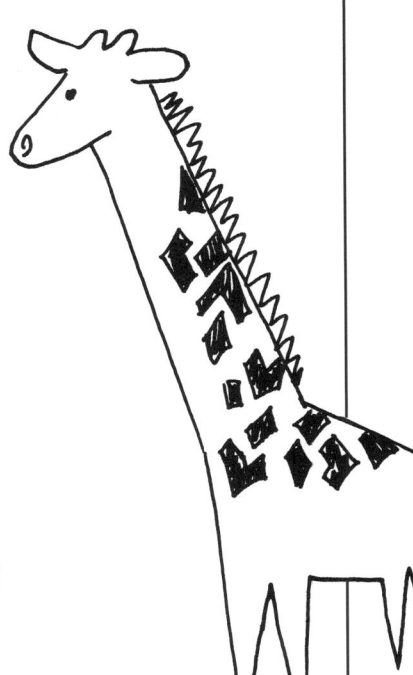

Would it work for you to drive me to the airport tonight?

Empathy & Understanding
"I imagine you're under a lot of stress from this trip and you'd like some support?"

Cooperation & Contribution
"Sure, I just need to run an errand on the way there."

How Giraffees **SAY "NO"**
(honesty connected to needs)

HOW JACKALS **HEAR "NO"**

HOW GIRAFFES **HEAR "NO"**

HABITUALLY

we listen to someone's pain
(emotional or physical) and then we

- sympathize
- give advice
- tell our own story
- invalidate
- interrogate
- educate

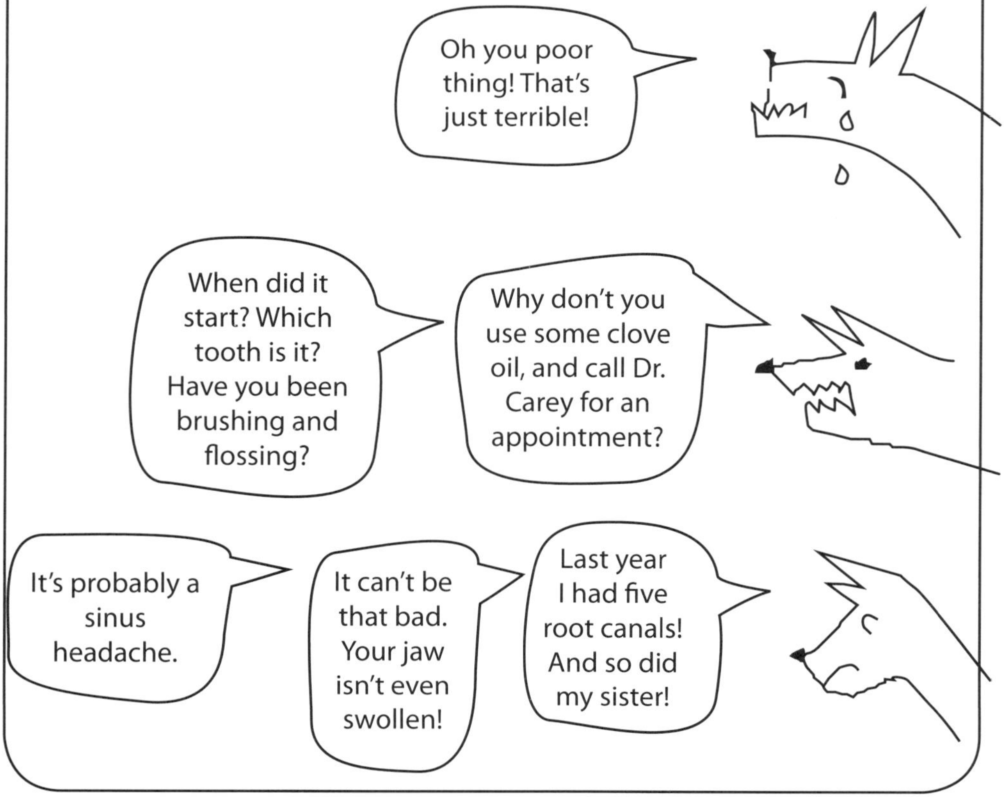

NATURALLY
we listen and then we

- connect with their feelings
- and needs
- and what they might want

Oh my tooth hurts!

Are you feeling scared because you want to know what's happening with your tooth?

Would you like to hear my suggestion?

Are you needing some relief so you can go to work?

It sounds so painful. Is there anything I can do?

Sounds like you're in a lot of discomfort.

JACKAL **SELF-TALK**
I blame, label, and judge myself

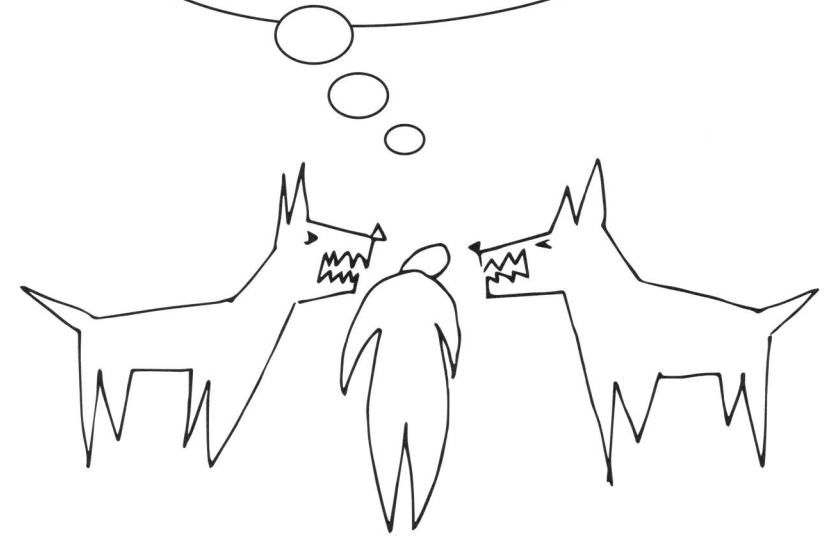

- I can't believe I did such a stupid thing!
- I'm letting everyone down.
- I'm worthless, I'll never get it right.
- I shouldn't have said that to him.
- I shouldn't have done that.
- I'm unlovable. No one could/does love me.
- I'm such a klutz!
- I ought to be more careful.
- I'm smarter than Zack.
- I'm a terrible (student, boss, friend, spouse, etc.)
- I never should have gotten up this morning.

GIRAFFE **SELF-EMPATHY**
I connect with my FEELINGS & NEEDS

- I'm feeling confused and I'm needing clarity.
- I feel annoyed and am wanting to be understood.
- I'd like support. I'm feeling sad today.
- It's important to me to be heard.
- I need to make my own choices in this situation.
- I like it when I feel cared for and comforted.
- I'm wanting compassion and connection.
- I can breathe and relax, and accept and value myself.
- I'm enjoying my ability to complete this challenging job.
- I'm appreciating my skills and knowledge.
- I'm happy I feel healthy and strong.

LISTENING WITH JACKAL EARS
habitual ways of silently judging and evaluating
self and others

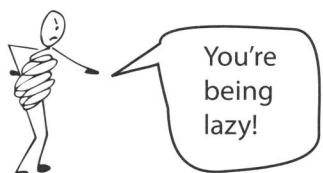

I know I should be more helpful and do more work around here. I'm just a lazy slob.

Who made YOU the boss?!

JACKAL **ears**
worn facing IN
(blaming self)

JACKAL **ears**
worn facing OUT
(blaming others)

LISTENING WITH GIRAFFE EARS
conscious ways to make a compassionate connection
in silence with self and with others

You're being lazy!

Whew! When I hear that I'm feeling sad and wanting some acknowledgment for all that I do around here!

GIRAFFE **ears**
worn facing IN
(connecting to self)

I wonder if they're feeling annoyed because they're wanting some help and cooperation?

GIRAFFE **ears**
worn facing OUT
(connecting to others)

JACKAL **REACTING**

Stimulus

- what someone does
- what someone says

Reaction

- takes it personally
- defends themself
- attacks and judges
- buttons get pushed

GIRAFFE **RESPONDING**

Stimulus

- what someone does
- what someone says

Response

- connection and empathy for self and others
- knows "it's not about me"
- seeks mutual understanding

JACKAL **POWER**
is unequal... "power over" (bully) or "power under" (victim)

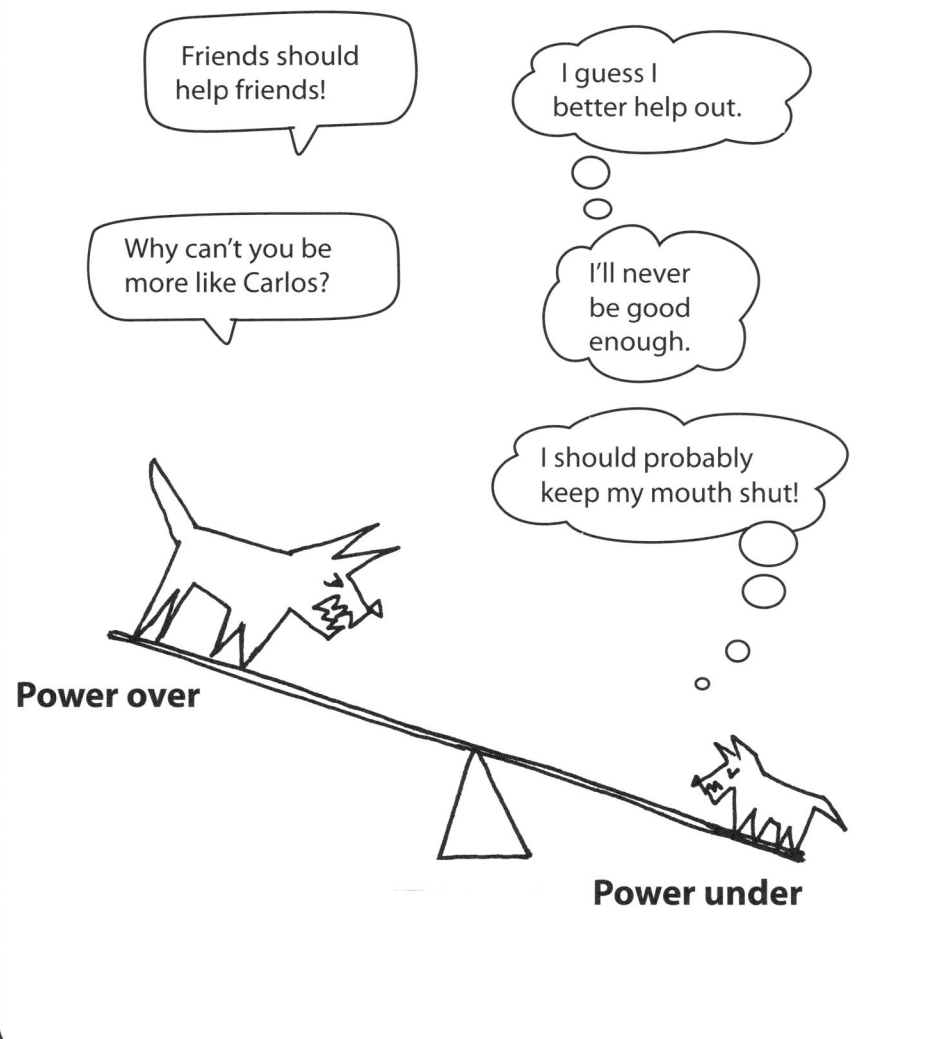

GIRAFFE **POWER**
is equal... "power with," or "win/win"

JACKAL **UNRESOLVED CONFLICT**

GIRAFFE **RESOLUTION OF CONFLICT**

GIRAFFE **ANGER**
connects with deeper feelings and needs

47

JACKAL "Life-defeating sentences"

GIRAFFE "Life-serving sentences"

I'm starting to notice when I'm enjoying what I'm doing or seeing.

I like it when I accomplish even something simple.

I can tell others what I'm willing and not willing to do.

It's OK to ask people for help and support.

49

JACKAL **APOLOGIES**

- promotes win/lose, good/bad, right/wrong, power over/under
- "I'm sorry" is expressed with guilt, or to "erase" personal responsibility

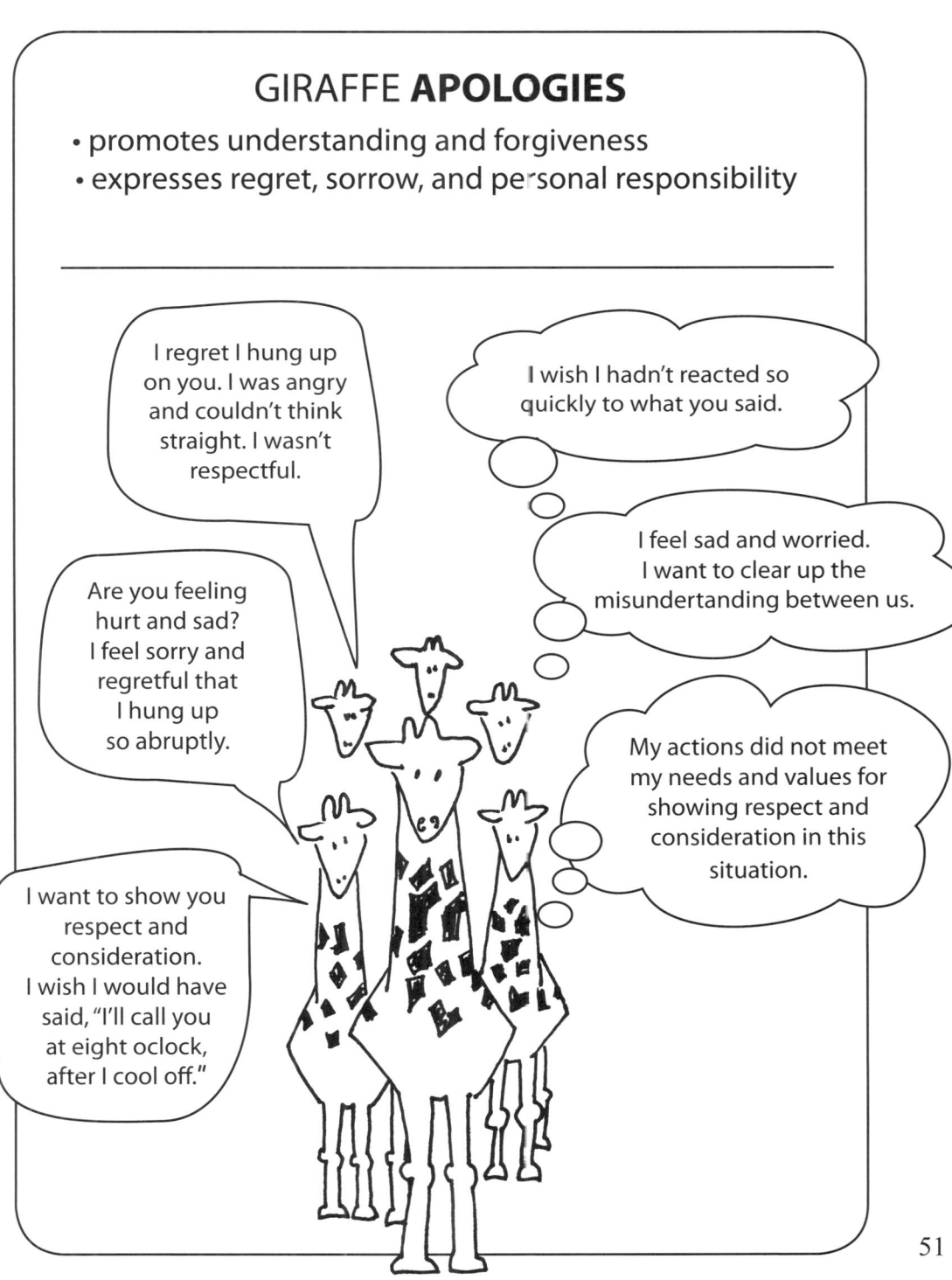

51

JACKAL **BRAGGING & BOASTING!**

GIRAFFE **CELEBRATION!**

JACKAL **COMPLAINING**
self-pity, whining, and wallowing

Now that Jack broke up with me, no one will ever ask me out again.

They cut my job and now I'll probably be unemployed for months.

I broke my stupid leg and now all my friends are going skiing without me.

GIRAFFE **MOURNING**
of losses, lost opportunities

I'm so sad Jack and I aren't together. I miss our connection and the fun we had.

What a disappointment! My job got cut! I was hoping it would last for years and years.

I'm bummed I can't get around easily and I'll miss going skiing with my friends.

JACKAL PRAISE & FLATTERY
judges, labels, and evaluates the other person

GIRAFFE **APPRECIATION & GRATITUDE**
expresses OBSERVATIONS, FEELINGS,
and how my life is enriched

I like the way your eyes sparkle when you laugh.

Wow! You made two goals!

I appreciate that you fed the puppies while we were on vacation.

I'm grateful you put gas in the tank! Now I can get to work on time.

JACKAL **PUNISHMENT**

•I want you to suffer.
• I want you to feel pain and/or guilt.
• I think if you feel pain you'll learn what's right
and what's wrong.
• You brought this on yourself.
• It's for your own good.
• I warned you!
• You should have known better.
• You should have listened to me.
• I want you to suffer like I've suffered;
then you'll know how I feel.

GIRAFFE **PROTECTIVE USE OF FORCE**

- My intention is to protect life.
- I value the health and safety
of you, me, and others.
- I will take action that has no intent to harm or punish -
only to protect.
- I did everything else I could before taking this action.

TRICKY JACKAL **STORMS**
to watch out for !

• You shouldn't be such a Jackal!
• That's a judgment!
• That's not really a feeling!
• I don't cause your pain!
• You've forgotten everything you know about Giraffe!

• I'm really being a big Jackal here -- but look who's talking!!
• I should be a Giraffe when he's being a jerk like this.
• I'm never going to be a Giraffe!
• I shouldn't have these Jackal thoughts!!

• You're supposed to be empathetic!
• What's your problem? Where are your Giraffe ears?!
• You should read that *Communications FUNdamentals* book again!

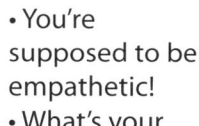

HA-HA!!

GIRAFFE **SUGGESTIONS**
to help calm the Jackal storms

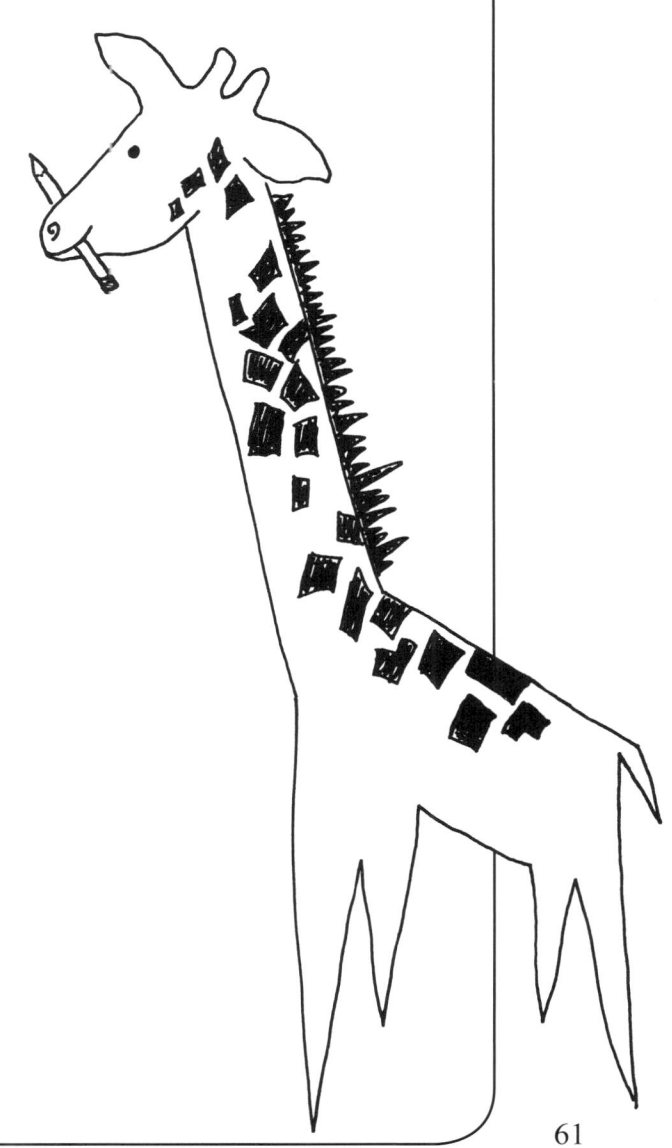

- ☒ take deep breaths
- ☒ relax tense muscles
- ☒ self-empathy
- ☒ ask for empathy
- ☒ write in journal
- ☒ sleep, rest, meditate
- ☒ take a "time in" for self-connection
- ☒ exercise
- ☒ throw a fully conscious Jackal tantrum

61

JACKAL PLAYING "GIRAFFE COP"

GIRAFFE **BEING GIRAFFE**

GIRAFFE **ACKNOWLEDGES CHOICE**
and connects with values & needs

> I'd like to stay home today

> I'm going to work to keep my goals and to respect myself.

> Even though ice cream would taste great...

> I'm choosing food that supports my health <u>and</u> tastes great!

> I value safety and I make sure my car has regular maintenance.

> I feel protective of the wild dolphins and want to honor the distance recommended by the marine biologists.

JACKAL **ENEMY IMAGES**

GIRAFFE

Get to the heart of what matters most.

Safety and consideration are really important to me.

I want our environment protected

I want to be with someone I trust.

I'm guessing autonomy and acceptance might matter to them.

GIRAFFE **CONNECTION GAME**

What we heard Marshall Rosenberg say about **JACKAL** habits

When we blame others we give up the power to change ourselves.

Jackal options when needs aren't getting met:
a. get angry and get results, fuel resentments and fear in others
b. get apathetic and feel awful and do nothing

Never hear what a jackal-speaking person thinks –
hear the (unspoken) need.

Any defensiveness or tightness I feel is my buying in to my own jackal
judgments/attacks…..so empathize with myself first.

Our body and spirit pays for it when we think Jackal.

Jackal: "I want you to guess what I want before I even know what it is,
and then always do it and always want to do it."

When you hear a jackal in their head (that's where their judgments come
from), go to their heart (their giraffe heart!) and guess their feelings and
needs. Place your attention there. Don't get caught up in their/my ideas
about things! That takes us to Jackal Land!

Marshall Rosenberg (1934 - 2015)

What we heard Marshall Rosenberg
say about **GIRAFFE** consciousness

"We can make life miserable or wonderful for ourselves and others depending upon how we think and communicate."

The objective of NVC is not to change people and their behavior in order to get our way; it is to establish relationships based on honesty and empathy which will eventually fulfill everyone's needs.

Needs ~ life energy calling to itself.

All the ways and times I wasn't able to "be giraffe" were my best teachers.

When to express empathy and when to express honesty:
Use empathy, even if silent, when we feel it would do one of three things:

1) when we sense a person needs affirmation

2) when we're not sure what was said and we want to hear accurately

3) when we sense the person has more to say, go deeper,
"let them take me on the trip". If I want to "take them on my trip",
I go to my expression, my honesty.

This model doesn't "prevent" miscommunication; but gives an opportunity to do something different when miscommunications happen.

Marshall Rosenberg (1934 - 2015)

JACKAL **BOOGIE**

We love to boogie and dance and sing;
our howls of attack have a familiar ring.
Remember these mean "please listen to me,"
and translate my message so we can now see
the beautiful needs, universally TRUE,
that live in ME and YOU and YOU!!

GIRAFFE **BOOGIE**

We hold open the invitation
to join our herd in celebration!
With frequent translations of any strife,
we keep connected to
the language of life!

Web Resources for Learning NVC

- **groktheworld.com,** where you can find materials and products for learning and teaching NVC

- **giraffeheartstuff.com,** Jean's website for more communication materials and whimsical giraffe stuff.

- **nvcsantacruz.org,** where you can find Jean's and co-facilitator's schedules of workshops, classes and retreats

- **cnvc.org** Center for Nonviolent Communication, a global organization featuring NVC information, international trainers, schedule of events, books, CDs, DVDs, and other materials

- **nvceducatorsinstitute.com** features information on Summer NVC Educators Institutes and specialized NVC training for educators

- **nonviolentcommunication.com,** a publisher of NVC books, cds, dvds; includes articles on NVC, and extensive list of quotes by Marshall Rosenberg

- **nvctraining.com,** a site to learn NVC through video clips and telecourses

About the Author

Jean enjoys...
❖her beach-town home
❖quality time with daughter, Kelly
❖projects, art, and fun with friends
❖ learning, reading, playing sports
❖making up games to play
with anyone willing
❖playing joyful boogie blues piano
❖teaching, counseling, and
creating NVC materials
❖staying healthy with daily doses
of nature and gratitude

Suggestions for using this book:
• Read it cover to cover while eating popcorn
• Write your notes in the margins
• Leave it lying around your house
for you and others to pick up and browse
• Give it to friends, family members,
and especially those who enjoy
illustrated books
• Color it
• Feel free to copy pages to use and share
(Please refrain from copying the entire book)

Acknowledgements

I have bountiful GRATITUDE
for contributions in the first edition from
Christine King (collaborating and editing);
expertise from Denny Brizendine (design),
Osa Sister (formatting), and LeAnn Meyer
(editing); and for ongoing support
from family and friends.

I've been buoyed from all the feedback
and appreciations I've received through the
years from happy readers of the first edition,
all of which prompted me to create this
second edition. I have joyfully completed it
with superb and magical help in formatting
from graphic designer Michelle Luedtke,
and editorial support by Nancy Barker that
resulted in my big, relaxing "ahhhh."

**Your comments, suggestions,
and stories are welcome!**

giraffe@cruzio.com

-- jean

Notes